techno craft

the work of Susan Cohn
1980 to 2000

■ national gallery of australia

Our appreciation is extended to the Directors and staff of the many public collecting institutions which have supported us with loans: National Gallery of Victoria, Melbourne; Art Gallery of South Australia, Adelaide; Art Gallery of Western Australia, Perth; City of Banyule Art Collection, Banyule City Council; Jewish Museum of Australia, Melbourne; State Craft Collection, Arts Victoria, Melbourne; Museum and Art Gallery of the Northern Territory, Darwin; Powerhouse Museum, Sydney; Queensland Art Gallery, Brisbane; Queen Victoria Museum & Art Gallery, Launceston. The enthusiastic support of Alessi s.p.a., Crusinallo (Italy), and in particular Anna Schwartz Gallery, Melbourne is acknowledged. I would especially like to thank all the individual lenders who have loaned their cherished and often most personal items of jewellery for this survey exhibition.

The contributors to this book have given their time most generously: the authors Jackie Cooper and Bruce James, the designer Garry Emery of Emery Vincent Design, the photographers Kate Gollings and Earl Carter, and the printers Toth Bienk & Associates.

I wish to pay tribute to the late Jim Logan, Curator of Australian Decorative Arts 1995 to 1998. His courage, despite serious illness, and his irrepressible good humour, made this exhibition happen. In his sad absence, the staff of the National Gallery of Australia have brought this project to fruition and I am grateful to all involved.

I would like to thank the artist Susan Cohn for creating such beautiful work and also for the valuable time and attention she and her Workshop 3000 team have given to the preparation and formation of this project. It has been a delight to work with them.

Brian Kennedy, Director, National Gallery of Australia

This publication accompanies the National Gallery of Australia's travelling exhibition *Techno Craft: the work of Susan Cohn 1980 to 2000* shown at:

National Gallery of Australia
Canberra, Australian Capital Territory
11 March to 18 June 2000

Brisbane City Gallery
Brisbane, Queensland
27 July to 10 September 2000

Object Galleries
Sydney, New South Wales
7 October to 19 November 2000

Venue to be confirmed
December 2000 to January 2001

Jam Factory Contemporary
Craft and Design
Adelaide, South Australia
17 February to 1 April 2001

Plimsoll Gallery
University of Tasmania
Hobart, Tasmania
27 April to 20 May 2001

Australian Centre
for Contemporary Art
Melbourne, Victoria
June to July 2001

preface

Susan Cohn is a craftsperson – jeweller, metalworker, designer – and an ardent modernist. Since 1980, Cohn has been working from her studio in the centre of Melbourne – appropriately named Workshop 3000. Over the past two decades Cohn has produced a large, diverse and consistent body of work which intersects engagingly with modern-day life.

Throughout her career, Cohn has looked beyond the conventions of precious jewellery and towards her immediate environment for ideas. Bamboo scaffolding in Hong Kong and venetian blinds from suburbia were early instances. Walkman headphones, security badges and hearing aids inspired another series. She has continually refined a set of reduced forms – the signature doughnut bracelets, sleek tableware shapes and the coolest condom holders – which are often made in non-precious anodised aluminum or steel. Each piece that Cohn makes interrogates the assumptions and meanings of jewellery and personal adornment. Nowhere is this more evident than in the installations – Reflections on A Safe Future and Way Past Real, for example – which have become an integral part of the artist's individual and production work.

The National Gallery of Australia has long played an important role in regard to contemporary art practice, both Australian and international. Techno Craft: the work of Susan Cohn 1980 to 2000 is the first survey of a contemporary jeweller and metalworker to be mounted by the National Gallery. The National Gallery of Australia has developed this project as a travelling exhibition with six interstate venues following its debut in Canberra. The exhibition features jewellery and tableware – both commercially produced and individually made pieces – as well as installation works. It is drawn from the National Gallery's collection, with numerous loans from Australian museums and public institutions, private collections as well as the artist herself.

This book includes three essays which meditate, firstly on the artist, secondly on her work and finally on the sadly absent progenitor of the project, the curator Jim Logan. The first essay teases out the personality behind the artist. In April 1999, Dr Brian Kennedy – Director of the National Gallery of Australia – interviewed Susan Cohn in her Melbourne studio. Brian Kennedy discovered a fascinating world in which Cohn's sharp and witty intellect mixes with heavy machinery, precision tooling and Techno music.

Jackie Cooper is an editor and writer on architecture and design. Cooper has been reflecting on and writing about the work of Susan Cohn from the very beginning of the artist's career. Her essay Susan Cohn – Jewellery: a typology examined combines an intimate knowledge of Cohn's oeuvre over two decades with insightful commentary on the broader social and cultural issues raised by the artist's work.

Jim Logan (1958–1998) curated this exhibition. Between 1995 and 1998, Jim was the extraordinarily gifted Curator of Australian Decorative Arts at the National Gallery of Australia. Jim's taste and humour have left an indelible mark on the exhibition in much the same way that he did through life.

Bruce James, an art critic and writer who had the privilege of being a close and long-time friend of Jim Logan, has penned a delightful tribute entitled The Dragonfly. Art and everyday life were inextricably linked in Jim's world. Bruce James' piece captures that effervescent talent of Logan's to illuminate decorative arts and design so intrinsically within the realm of contemporary art practice, as with his last curatorial project – this survey of work by Susan Cohn.

Roger Leong, National Gallery of Australia

material girl
living in a material world

Brian Kennedy

Let me take you inside Susan Cohn's workshop. I've never been in a jeweller's workshop like it, and am fascinated to record the array of objects, materials, colours and books before me.

Pipe stands, bowls, insects, spectacles. Books: *Africa Adorned, Coins, Gold of Africa, Jewels of the Pharoahs, Anatomy for the Artist, The Sense of Order, Buttons, Machinist*. The door of a safe, what's inside? *Colour Charts*, all coded, a mirror. CDs: Leonard Cohen, Lou Reed, Nick Cave, Laurie Anderson, kd lang, Tom Waites. Slides, earrings. A personal computer, computer disks, files, perforations, ring boxes, vices, big machines, small machines. *Critical Safety Rules:* 'Tie Hair Back', 'Wear Goggles and Mask', 'Use Proper Lighting'.

Susan Cohn calls herself a craftsperson but one who shifts across boundaries: 'I wanted to be known as a craftsperson because of the tradition the work comes from. Perhaps it slides into visual arts, but I think the nature of the object, the play of the ideas, where they're coming from, and what they're being used for is still very much bound within the tradition of craft. I think it shifts into design too. The work doesn't sit very comfortably solely in one area.'

Her studio is an Aladdin's cave, a wonderful experience for the uninitiated. She is focussed on the present day with an eye to the future, and her visual references to the past are deeply embedded so that they never interfere with our perception of her modernism. She gives us joy and that encourages us not to take ourselves or her work too seriously. She believes in the necessity of humility and has the confidence to wear it. 'I think we often forget how educated our audience is. And people like to be offered a different way of wearing something and different ideas. So I try to offer that, rather than saying, well I think this is popular at the moment, I'll provide that. Maybe the only exception is colour, I might use colour sometimes in that sense to mark moments in life.'

When I first saw the work of Susan Cohn, presented to me by the irrepressible and sadly departed Jim Logan, I wanted to know this craftsperson jeweller with a sense of humour. Susan Cohn makes no apology – and often sets out to provoke: 'I think it's a very interesting way to communicate and to make someone laugh. I think irony is a fantastic way to play, to make people think, react or respond – but there should be some humour in there.' But she never allows the humour to become attention seeking: 'I think I have some very good critics around me who protect me from trying to be too smart and I rely on them to do that, and also you keep editing yourself. I think it's really important.'

Fundamentally, Susan Cohn is a communicator. She thinks about the people who wear her jewellery. She insists that all her jewellery can be worn, and she tests it first on herself. This is a profound and essential message in her work: 'Jewellery is about people. The work is about people, so it's really important to keep that perspective. It is too easy to get caught up in the nature of the object itself and forget that the fundamental purpose of jewellery is to be worn.'

It has always been that there are people who like to wear objects on their body, and those who prefer to be naked. I have always been in the latter category, my one concession to jewellery is my gold wedding ring. But Susan Cohn has me interested. She may yet tempt me to seek to adorn, decorate and embellish my body with jewellery. Her work invites a tactile response. She engages with your senses in a way that invites attention. She explains: 'Take the doughnut bracelet as an example: the size and the scale of it are really important. Once you start to deal with scale and you think about the size of it, its roundness and lusciousness, you need to touch it. I think my forms are playing with the sensual quality of the object.' The jewellery of Susan Cohn is indeed sensual. It needs touching and invites entering and probing.

The pursuit of a university doctorate, the keen intelligence which begets her work, is rooted in a caring and a yearning for articulation about jewellery usage: 'My work can be considered in an art gallery and it can also be worn on someone's arm. The work still has the same value regardless of context, yet I think craft keeps separating the two. This is a fascinating area that I like to explore.'

The invitation of an expert jeweller who cares in the way Susan Cohn does, is an invitation to explore with one's senses. Susan Cohn has always known her own predilection: 'I've always been a tactile person and was always interested in making things. I think that's why the suggestion of my going into jewellery was originally attractive. I didn't want to stay in graphics, and someone said, you should do jewellery, you're always making comments and observations about it, thinking interesting things about it, and I thought, oh yeah why not. Six months into my course, I knew this was it. As a child I would always make things. I got into trouble for taking the clock apart because I wanted to know how it worked and I was always playing with things that could be worn.'

The curiosity of mind which is so obvious in the work of Susan Cohn indicates a fondness for numerology: 'Oh yes. I like numbers, I like logic, I like puzzles, yes definitely. Very early in my career I became interested in numbers. Even my early one-off pieces, like the stone brooch in the NGA collection, played with the idea of multiples.'

The workshop seems so quiet. I am acutely aware of the silence in this place. 'Yes it is a silent place to work, frequently one of calm, the silence allows us to hear the noise of making. Sounds like music.' But at other times the music of the machinery is enhanced by recordings: 'Yes, with certain work. We put on blues, jazz, reggae, dance music, a whole range of music, whatever fits the job we are doing. Other times when you need company, you need to hear lyrics and you need to listen to Nick Cave and those sort of people.'

Jewellery is challenging work requiring endless patience: 'So much of it is routine. But so much of every job is routine. You have to find some way in which to move your way through the work and enjoy the making, the polishing, the finishing. A lot of jewellery work fails because to do it properly is mundane and boring. To me it's thinking time, it's fantastic. I know what I'm doing and I'm still enjoying finishing the work properly.'

Susan Cohn is very clear about the two lines of her exhibition work: 'There's one line which is like the *Way Past Real* and *Catch Me* series which talks about production and about making something unique out of something that's a multiple. The other line of work is the *Cosmetic Manipulations* series, where the work talks about how we wear things, and draws on traditional work. *Cosmetic Manipulations* comes more from ethnic traditional culture where age is signified by the markings on the face or the wearing of jewellery. Both these concerns cross over, and I try to alternate them, because the *Cosmetic Manipulations* work is tough and people find it very hard to relate to. So I use familiar things such as multiples quite deliberately because they are more accessible, and my work isn't just about being tough. But the ideas are always there.'

The research behind the jewellery of Susan Cohn is obvious. Take the insects: 'Yes, I did a lot of research on insects, loved it. Again it's about taxonomy: numbers and multiples and species. I love all that sort of side of it, subtle differences. But it's also that the insects are very elegant, almost fragile, beautiful looking things that can be quite dangerous and I like that.'

While adamant that she is a craftsperson and vocal that 'craftsperson' is not a derogatory term but one of which she is proud, Susan Cohn is also certain that she is not a sculptor. She does however give serious thought and concentration to installations of her work: 'I think I've always used installation as a means of expression and communicating ideas because I hated jewellery exhibitions. I hated craft shows, I hated showcases and just objects being plonked down. It was so removed from the people coming to look at the show. So in my first exhibition I consciously allowed people to pick up the work and try it on. I've always been interested in exhibition design and this goes back to my graphic training with Garry [Emery]. I was taught to look at the way in which things were presented, like how to capture completely different moods. It was certainly never an idea of making a sculpture, it was about using the space which the work was in to express the spirit of the work. That's what I always try to achieve.'

After just a few years in Australia, a few observations come to my mind about the situation of craft in the country. One is that its excellence is obvious, but its practitioners are often so defensive. Susan Cohn is focussed internationally, but has chosen to operate from Melbourne. She is in the vanguard of those exceptional artists who embrace and rejoice in their viability in the commercial arena: 'Well when I first started, I made this conscious decision that I wanted to make a living from my work. Initially, of course, I had to find other means of support until I developed a business. The other thing that happens in Australia is that if people want to make things work internationally, they feel they must go to live overseas. I sort of became obsessed with trying to make it work from here. It was much harder and it was going to take longer, but there had to be a way in which you could do it. The more of us that do it, the more it can work.'

Any discussion with Susan Cohn, a visit to her workshop, and time spent in her exhibitions, must evoke, provoke and stimulate an interest in contemporary Australian jewellery. Susan Cohn is studying managed identity for her doctoral thesis. She is concerned about how we manage our different identities today: 'Take clothing and jewellery – jewellery will tell you more than clothing. I am looking at jewellery as a cultural signifier, looking at street culture, gay culture, different types of small in-group cultures, where jewellery has been used in that sense. I am also looking at the medical body, cosmetic surgery – that's where the *Cosmetic Manipulations* pieces come from. I also find it really interesting to look at where jewellery keys into the future, what jewellery might be in the future, especially how it grows out of technology.'

Susan Cohn – you have got me hooked. I am interested, fascinated and absorbed. Your engaging personality is at the heart of your work. It will speak long after you are gone, and will be celebrated by everyone who has the opportunity to wear your jewellery. Joie de vivre, continue to thrive, material girl, craftsperson. I give her the last word: 'I choose to be more provocative and maybe a little bit naughty. Life's too short to just let everything slide past you, I mean it's so easy to do that.'

Aluminium rivets, glues, fire extinguishers, blow lamps, heavy duty granular hand cleanser. Pickle, rows and rows of orange juice bottles. Colours: emerald, lush green, forget-me-not blue, violet, bordeaux, purple black, fake gold, sunflower yellow, salmon pink, edo purple, turquoise. An anodising room, 'Use a mask if necessary', 'Wear gloves and coat', 'Cover acid especially when in use'. Rubber gloves, hose, extractor. Folding boxes, different size files, emery sticks, needle files, saw blades, punches, pliers, herbal tea. Chenier vice, leather pouch, spring tweezers. Books: *Easy Exercises for a Better Memory, Dictionary of Symbols, Plastic as an Art Form, Silversmithing*. Metal working, artist anodising aluminium. Susan Cohn stretches boundaries.

Brian Kennedy, Director, National Gallery of Australia

All quotes from discussion with Susan Cohn on 9 April 1999

jewellery
a typology examined

Jackie Cooper

Ideas are central in Susan Cohn's work. When she makes something, it is with a proposition in mind that extends beyond the functional and aesthetic concerns of designing an object or an artefact. These propositions are that value is not situated in material preciousness and fine craftsmanship alone; that jewellery might be accessible, not elitist, and it might embody social messages; and that serially-produced objects might be made as important and individually distinctive as one-offs.

She sets out to explore and extend the typology of jewellery. Her tactics include transgressing the codes of what is decorative, inflating scale, investing objects with meaning, and irony. Her aim is to push the limits of the definition of jewellery and yet preserve its core role of adornment by making objects that can be worn on the body.

Typically Cohn uses street culture for design inspiration, observing how people appropriate everyday articles to wear in decorative and status-denoting or cultural ways: spectacles, security passes, key rings; and also how technological, mass-produced artefacts such as headphones can acquire decorative and emblematic power – qualities that are the essence of jewellery. She even takes as a starting point for design orthodontic braces.

Her work, with its stark functionalist aesthetic and fastidious detailing, is strongly motivated by pleasure in the play of form, material and colour. Materials are juxtaposed unexpectedly and ideas collide to release humour and irony. The objects invariably surprise.

Cohn draws no distinctions in hierarchy of importance between exhibitions, commissions or production work. She uses them all for experimenting and for developing ideas, and they all, in turn, inform each other.

Ideologically, the production work is central to the way she operates, because it permits popular series such as the doughnut bracelets and the interchangeable disc earrings. Being less labour-intensive, these are less expensive than one-off commissions: democratic jewellery. But they also have another significance as the site for technical and conceptual experimentation.

The serially-produced bracelets – all formed from an identical mould – owe their individuality to distinctions in materials, joining details and surface treatments. Cohn has produced a 'history line' of twenty different doughnut bracelets, representing twenty years of practice. These include the *Bound* series (1982–), with 'primitive' moccasin binding generating a polemical reading of the hand-made one-off and the machine-made mass-produced artefact. In the *Flyaway* series (1984–), an aluminium mesh frill denies the practicality of the join and ironically expresses the material. The *Stonewash* series (1984–) picks up on fashion's fetish for denim, the distressed surface suggesting a patina of age and producing another kind of associative value beyond the aesthetic or precious values of jewellery. The *Saw* series (1985), with its zig-zag edges, evokes Memphis graphics. The *Bullethole* series (1987–) exploits the visual pleasures of layering solid and perforated aluminium, the play of different colours and the sliding collisions of mesh. The *Torn Mesh* series (1988) responds to a punk aesthetic of making value out of something destroyed. The clear plastic *Survival* series (1998–) shares with the black aluminium *Slot* series (1999–) an interest in exploiting the interior hidden space of the doughnut – the *Survival* bracelet using the entire hollow volume and the *Slot* bracelet hiding little geometric compartments.

The doughnut bracelets invoke Moholy-Nagy's idea of using 'reproductive apparatuses' for productive purposes (i.e., to make 'originals'): the artefact created by the techniques of mass production yet hand-finished or otherwise made unique.

The exhibition, *Way Past Real* (1994), rationally dissects this polemic of authentic/fake and original/copy, and highlights too Cohn's central question: where does value lie? The exhibition groups 153 apparently identical gold doughnut bracelets in four families. Conceptually they all deal with authenticity, fakes, coding, value, and vanity. But each family highlights certain key ideas.

In the group of 24 carat gold-plated bracelets, a single bracelet is 24 carat pure gold – but visually you can't tell the 'real' one. Similarly in the family of gold anodised bracelets, you can't tell which one is the 'original' made by Cohn, as distinct from the others made by the Workshop 3000 team. The third family is raw polished aluminium convincingly lit to look as though gold; the illusion evaporates as soon as the bracelets are removed from the lighting – and yet these are not fakes. A fourth family of bracelets has different surface treatments, all gold, but with no effort to look 'genuine'. In its lack of pretence, this constitutes the most 'honest' family.

In *Way Past Real*, Cohn examines where the fake crosses the line, where it becomes validated, and what is more real than the real.

This exhibition also demonstrates the way that production work can become the focus of conceptual exploration, and it highlights the significance of the doughnut bracelet in Cohn's work. The doughnut was developed in the early 1980s. It was originally planned in silver, but she realised that aluminium was a better material: it is light, which improves wearability, it easily takes colour, and it can be pressed. By pressing, rather than using time-consuming gold- and silver-smithing techniques, she could raise a basic shape quickly. Anodised aluminium became her favoured material, and the doughnut bracelets the first of the serially-produced works: a repetitive form individualised through different joining techniques and surface treatments.

The turning point that enabled this decision towards serial production was a series of anodised aluminium louvre brooches. In using aluminium Cohn gained an understanding of its potential for serial production. The louvre brooches were her first aluminium works; they, in turn, grew directly out of a stone louvre brooch begun in 1980 while she was still a student. It had required a painstaking process first to cut each tiny serpentine louvre, then to drill the one-millimetre holes at 45 degrees to take the silver tubing – and she also had to construct the tools necessary for each stage of the delicate surgery.

The stone louvre brooch was in the elitist jewellery tradition of the one-off piece (while paradoxically making reference to a mass-produced, machined precision venetian blind). It was an extreme exercise in technique, and Cohn was also playing with material and form. In the same spirit, she experimented with material and form in the marble rings and triangular rings in coloured golds and blackened silver, made at the same time, 1980 to 1981, and also the bamboo scaffolding brooches of 1981 that formally derive from the stone brooch. In all these early works she was exploring the limits of jewellery, testing and transgressing conventional boundaries of reference, beauty, material, form, and yet maintaining a salient characteristic of jewellery: to be wearable.

Cohn's commitment to serial production generated the *Compressed brooch* series (1984–), a machine, serially-produced bar brooch made with a simple press tool conceptually based on the scrap metal industry's car compaction machines. The two narrow bars are bound with plastic hair ties. A ring-pull pin attaches the brooch to clothing. The compressed brooch sprang from an idea to use up coloured aluminium scrap left over from the anodising process. Each one, although fabricated by a mass-production technique, is individual. Men, as well as women, wear them, eroding a conventional jewellery gender taboo.

Since first making jewellery in 1980, Cohn has consistently explored the idea that value extends beyond material preciousness and craftsmanship to encompass the personal, emotional and associative qualities that often attach to jewellery. The black series of compressed brooches (1988–) is the first coherent resolution of this idea of ephemeral value: fragments of actual gold and silver jewellery (such as rings, cuff links) are embedded in the crushed aluminium scrap, introducing a poignant and personal memory value to each piece. (Ironically, the 'real' jewellery is destroyed in the process.)

The value that accrues over time in jewellery through the accumulation of private memories and feelings is the theme of the *Sheath* rings. In these fat rings, precious metal – silver or gold – is hidden inside a sleeve of aluminium. Cohn reverses the usual practice of plating a lesser metal with a thin veneer of something more costly. Inversion is typical of the way she communicates an idea in design. Here it is a means to house a secret. Sue Rowley has observed that Cohn hides, displaces or subverts something precious in order to create a protection for it. The inner secret, or preciousness, of the ring is revealed only after years of wear, as the aluminium skin progressively disintegrates. This process crucially relies on the wearer's own life experiences, endowing the ring with a value gained through intimate personal association and memory; and, paradoxically, what would normally be considered as defects – the dings and bashes inflicted on the aluminium – make each ring distinct, further adding to its personal significance and value.

Similarly, the overscaled chunky black aluminium *Scim* rings – developed in 1998 initially as a mourning ring after the death of Jim Logan – register the dents and scuff marks of daily life, and over time the glossy black surface wears thin. Time is incorporated as an active agent, bestowing an alternative order of value on the rings.

Value through association is also a theme in the 1989 exhibition, *...and does it work?*. People use everyday objects in decorative ways, i.e., like jewellery. Security passes, key rings, cellular phones all have potential as personal adornment and signifiers of power or membership of a group. Cohn perceives too the decorative potential of hearing aids, radio microphones, antennae, hospital bracelets, even builders' tools, as jewellery. Here she subjects the typology jewellery to close scrutiny: the ultimate determination of jewellery is whether or not an object has a use. In being functional, the most beautifully wrought silver watch or belt buckle is excluded from the category of jewellery. By stripping useful objects of their functionality and transforming them into jewellery, *...and does it work?* goes to the core of this typological condition.

The briefcase (1987) is perhaps the most extreme example of a functional object transformed into jewellery. Its tilted rectangular shape in black perforated aluminium parodies the racing businessman. With 150 separate bits, each individually crafted, it is a technically exacting work. The briefcase barely accommodates A4 paper, its uselessness an ironic, teasing commentary.

...and does it work? grew out of *Walkman #1* made in 1984; it exploits the decorative potential of headphones commonly worn by urban commuters. *Walkman #2* (1989) extends the literal formal replication of technology to suggest darker references too. The piece can be worn on the head à la headphones or around the neck or folded as a lapel brooch. In this latter guise the little gold 'earphones' become an insect's bulbous eyes. The slightly menacing metamorphosis from technology to creature ('technology breeds insects') is fully developed in the 1995 *Gibsonia* series. Cohn's interest in metamorphosis is evident in several works, sometimes as a simple transformation (wearing pieces in different ways on different parts of the body: *Cosmetic Manipulations*, *Out of Line* orthodontic jewellery), sometimes through reference (*Gibsonia*), and sometimes through the formal modification of the piece (*Walkman #2*).

The 1992 exhibition, *Cosmetic Manipulations*, examines people's obsession with appearance and is a critique of contemporary canons of beauty. The delicate gold and aluminium pieces are designed to be worn on the face, in fact to draw attention to the defects of age: crows' feet and baggy eyes, slack jowls and double chins, furrowed foreheads, batty ears. Delicate little metal jaws nip and tuck excess flesh, pull folds taut and smooth, hold the aging face in check.

The pieces are more redolent of prosthetic instruments than jewellery. They highlight the issues of vanity and the cult of youth, and offer a challenge to flout conventional standards of beauty by celebrating, not denying, one's lines of wisdom and experience. This arresting jewellery invites humour. The joke is intricately wrought: tiny meticulous mechanisms fashioned from yellow gold with pink gold springs and rivets and brightly coloured trailing aluminium wires. However, each piece can also be worn off the face, more conventionally attached to clothing, transforming the meaning of the work.

Another question of value is inherent in the 1995 exhibition, *Reflections on A Safe Future*. Here it is the value in being able to say yes or no to sexual overtures – a power conveyed by the talismanic force of the dragonfly/condom holder as well as by its practical function of containing protection. The work extends the etiquette of safe sex and personal choice.

Reflections is a collection of 45 pieces in seven groups of species: a taxonomy of dragonfly/talismans ranged according to colour and body shape. Each insect perches on a doughnut container designed to carry condoms. The pieces are hung round the neck on long wires.

The highly-reflective iridium-coated plutonite wings of the dragonflies are Oakley sunglass lenses – found objects – metamorphosed. The sinister insect form draws on past associations and archetypes. Its most potent formal reference is the dragonfly/woman corsage designed by Lalique in 1897. In this Art Nouveau piece, an insect undergoes transformation into a woman: she is a paradox of fragility and strength. In much of her work, Cohn expresses such paradoxes: organic/mechanical; beautiful/grotesque; powerful/fragile; secret/overt; protective/menacing; poignant/assertive; life/death. These oppositions give *Reflections* its tension and meaning.

Reflections is jewellery with a cause. In it Cohn seeks to imbue jewellery with a direct social message. The impetus comes from street culture, a principal generator of ideas since her earliest works. In her early pieces, she translates observations of street life directly: the series of aluminium pencils (1987) is prompted by observations of how pencils are worn tucked behind ears. The *Tag* series (1982) is made with nylon and mimics clothes labels. A pin (1992) resembling an arm of a pair of glasses is designed to be worn on a pocket. These pieces disturb expectations of what jewellery is and suggest alternative ways and places on the body to wear it; they also successfully cross gender barriers. But in later works deriving from street culture, such as the *Cohndom* box and *Survival Habits*, Cohn goes further than observe: these works contain social messages with profound implications.

The *Cohndom* box that first appeared in the *Reflections* exhibition became a production piece: often production work starts out like this as exhibition work, or vice versa. Made in pressed metal – aluminium or fine silver – or moulded plastic, the *Cohndom* box is light, portable, discreet, non-gender-specific, and designed for vending machines. It was selected in 1997 by Alessi as part of its range, and is the second piece designed by Cohn to be mass-produced by Alessi. The first is the *Cohncave* bowl that Alessi has manufactured since 1992. Mass-produced in layers of black and silver perforated steel, each bowl has a unique moiré signature created by the two layers of mesh.

The precursor to the *Cohncave* bowl is a limited edition of 50 smaller fruit bowls (1988–). These are made from two layers of perforated aluminium secured at the outer edge by a thin rim of gold or silver. The distinctive moiré patterns and different colour combinations generate individuality. The mesh bowls were Cohn's first tableware pieces – aside from a production series of aluminium cocktail glasses from 1984.

Mesh has a natural association with food, recalling the old-fashioned meat safe. The *Cohnical Phase* bowls followed the mesh fruit bowls, a series of containers of varying shapes and sizes in two layers of pressed aluminium mesh. Here the game has been to make an industrial material 'organic'. The mesh is stretched and moulded, creating dramatic moiré effects. From a distance the bowls produce the illusion of being solid, whereas close up, the disparity between the inside and outside forms is revealed. In *Cohnical Phase V*, which is 500mm in diameter, this disparity produces a formal tension where the internal yellow cone hovers just above the shallow flat black base.

In the exhibition *Catch Me* (1998), Cohn concentrates strictly on the typology jewellery. The exhibition is a transgressive act in which jewellery is examined in a purely self-referential way: there are no extraneous references or metaphors. The works are made entirely from the common bolt ring catches that secure most necklaces, the very parts of jewellery that are never meant to be the centre of attention. Here they are the entire story. In one work, 10,000 bolt ring catches are joined in a continuous chain measuring 100 metres, the sheer abundance of the humble elements transforming their meaning and rendering them significant, decorative and valuable. At a practical level, the chains can be purchased by the metre and worn at whatever length the wearer desires.

The exhibition *Survival Habits* (1999) develops the idea of the *Cohndom* box as a survival kit for the future, projecting ahead to 2020. While still containing a condom, *Survival Kit #2* also includes a series of essential devices and substances. For instance, there is a tiny 18 carat gold and aluminium brain jack, which is all that we will need to interface with any computer and download whatever information we need: the site of the brain jack will become a new site for jewellery. A phial of memory perfume contains a scent with a special meaning for the wearer: perhaps the smell of the sea, or of cigarettes (a lot of smells are likely to disappear in the next century). A nasal strip for easing difficult breathing will also help in smelling the memory perfume. There is a miniature gold hearing device, since telephones will become redundant. And a single tablet of a wonder drug will cure anything, but can only be taken once. All these magical commodities are packed into a *Cohndom* box that can be pocketed or worn round the neck.

Cohn stretches the typology: predictive jewellery.

Briefcase   Compressed brooch

the dragonfly

Jim Logan Necktag

'I heard a fly buzz when I died'
Emily Dickinson, 1862
'Gidday, Slag. How're they hanging?'
James Anthony Logan, 1998

Bruce James

It was not the attractiveness of decorative art that Jim Logan understood as its paramount quality. Nor even its practicality. What he understood was its necessity. Naturalness, I suppose, is the better word. That decorative art might be fanciful, indulgent or somehow inessential never occurred to him. Jim experienced jewellery – and fabrics, furniture, food, couture, cut or cultivated blooms, liqueurs, charge cards and sharp-edged conversation – as the expression of a biological imperative. Wearing a brooch, like arranging a Gymea lily with its flower-head just so, or making *risotto con funghi* from scratch, derived less from artifice than atavism.

The hoary quip about accessories serving to differentiate humans and animals assumed the status of a faith in him. The Amex company was an unsuspecting accomplice in Jim's mission to redecorate the world, or at least that region of it which he could sensibly plan to colonise in a career.

Yet wholly human as Jim was, an additional gene quotient tipped his being toward hybridity. The order to which he tended was that of the insects. Lepidoptera, perhaps. Or Odonata. What else explains the multi-jointed carapace of his body, articulated for defence, or the zig-zag operations of his thoughts? Hovering unswattably in one's face, he was a spectacle and an irritant. A conscience. We make shapes in life as we live it. Jim's was fashioned with all the concern for formal finish of the crafted objects in his charge. Even now, I run my hands along the prickled ridges, the eccentric flanges and filiaments of the unforgettable contour he carved for himself.

That such a creature found himself the Curator of Australian Decorative Arts at the National Gallery of Australia was necessary and natural too. Jim Logan flourished in the position. Wings he already possessed, of course, but in Canberra he spread them – a set of iridescent ailerons for which Susan Cohn's sunglass reprise on Lalique might have been the prototype. Sickened with the diseases that crushed and extinguished him in June, 1998, Jim devoted his final months to the preparation of the present exhibition of her work. Conceived as a testament to Cohn, it was also – and he knew this recklessly, ruthlessly – a self-portrait of a dragonfly in its death.

Toward the end, Jim teeter-tottered in plastic socks to catch the blood. His constant wisecracking, equally prophylactic, caught up all the other pain. When he could no longer staunch Death with a ribbon in this way, he died. I believe an element of aesthetic choice attended him at that moment. Opinionated to the last, he loosened his hold on life precisely when he could not regulate it as a *Composition with Emblems of Superior Taste*.

What was living, anyway, without power to gather a Liz Williamson scarf in ruffles at his neck, or clamp a Cohn creation to his torso like an amulet? The dumbest thing I ever did was to advise Greg Ralph, Jim's partner, against sending him to the flames wearing articles by each practitioner. For this Presbyterian scruple, I will doubtless be punished by him later.

Jim relished Cohn's art, grasping her importance from a very early point. In 1988, I recall, he enthused to his colleagues about her designs at the Contemporary Jewellery Gallery in Sydney. Later, he must have been one of the first in Australia to purchase her Alessi *Cohncave*, a high-table compote with a case of street-smarts. Unfailingly generous, he bought it for a friend, not himself. Loving it deeply, he loved the giving of it more. His advocacy of artworks was inseparable from his affection for artists, indeed for anyone who could demonstrate their ownership of *elan vital*.

Woe betide you, however, if you measured up short of the life force.

Extolling the technical construction and moiré elegance of the *Cohncave*, Jim was a study in holiest connoisseurship. Holding it up to the light for all of us to see, he could have been elevating the host, or proferring the dark disc of a fly's eye monumentalised as a totem. It wasn't enough simply to apprehend such a piece. One had to feel it. Embrace it, really. Jim was the last of the tactile curators of the twentieth century. A fruit bowl was a utensil right enough, but it was also the fruit itself, the consumable – and, once again, necessary and natural – manifestation of a living mind.

Though he enjoyed and collected paintings, their untouchability frustrated him. Touch was his aesthetic mainstay. Foolproof – yet mysterious, too. In terms of Cohn's productions, this meant he handled everything of hers that came his way with a physicality bordering on the erotic. Her pristine surfaces invited tactility, of course, but Jim's literalist version of the laying on of hands went beyond the boundaries of curatorship. Bodies or bowls, Jim couldn't keep his mits off if he tried – not that he ever did. His fingers did the walking, the talking and every imaginable action besides.

Amongst his proudest possessions was an example of the anodised ID tags Cohn produced in the mid nineties. You can see him flaunting it, Logan style, in a photograph taken by Kate Gollings for Cohn's survey catalogue, and reproduced here. Plate number one, as you'd expect. He's leaning into the page, the way he leaned into rooms, into conversations, into lives. The pendant, an industrial melding of plane and perforation, counterbalances his bending but does not lessen the likelihood of flight. Art, after all, was his wing.

Stone louvre brooch
Stone louvre brooch

Scaffolding brooch #2

Marble rings

Scaffolding brooch #1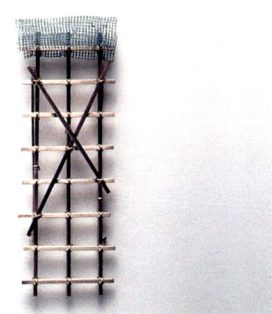

Straw bracelet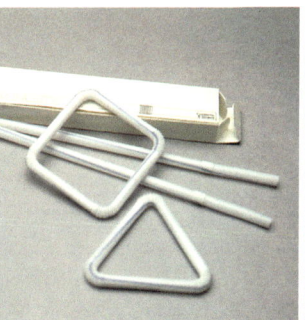

Tag brooches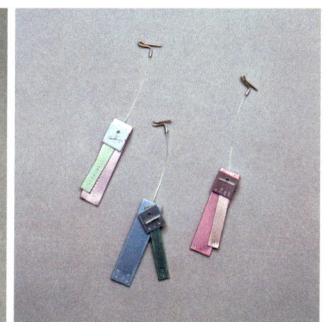

Louvre brooch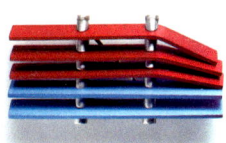

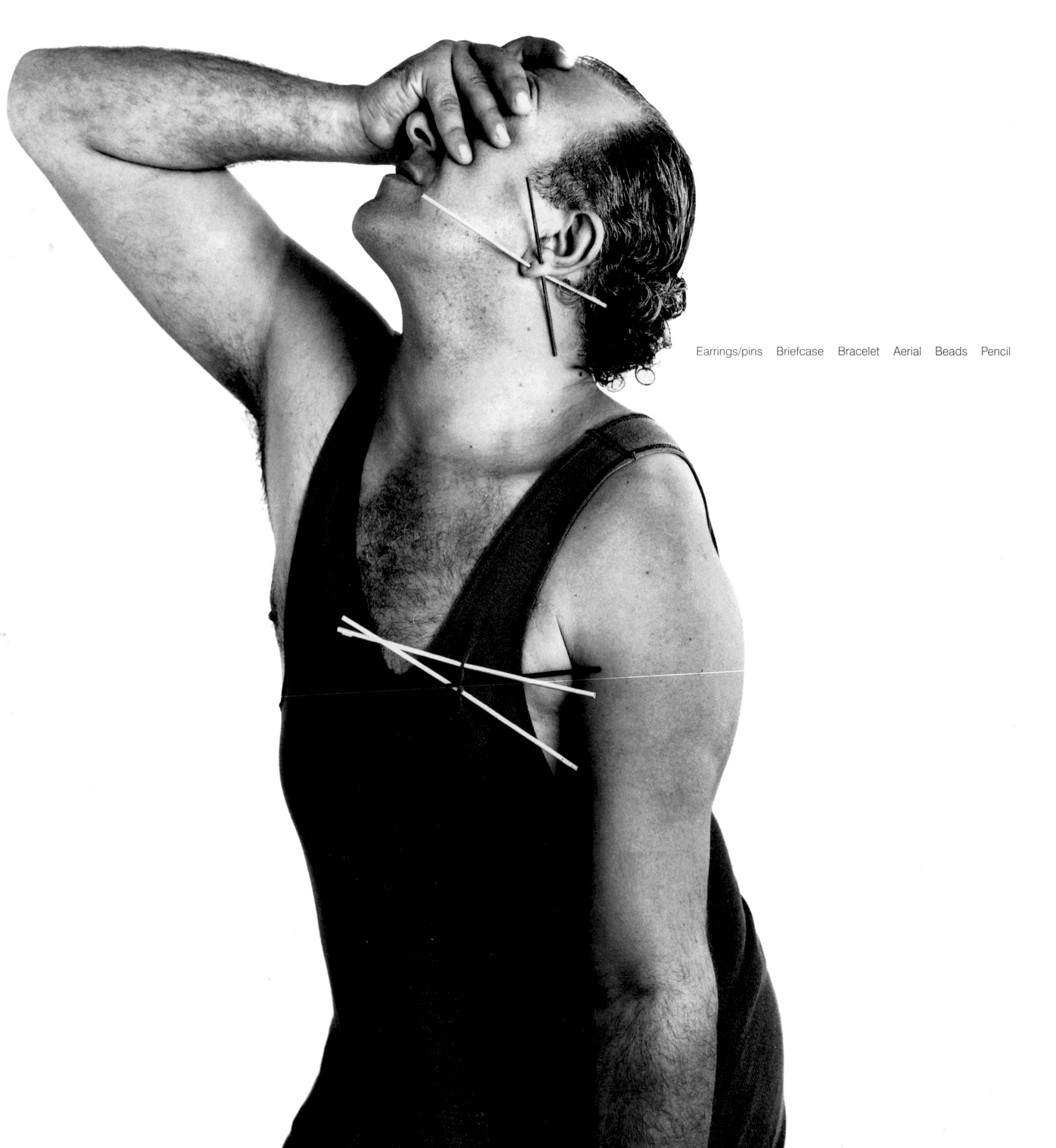

Earrings/pins Briefcase Bracelet Aerial Beads Pencil

early work
02

production work
bracelet 01

Slot
Torn Mesh
Flyaway
Bullet hole
Stonewash
Bound
Plastic
Half-torn

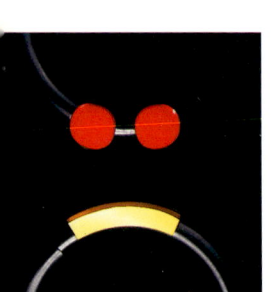

production work 02

Scim rings Earrings
Pins Cocktail glass
Compressed brooches Cohndom boxes

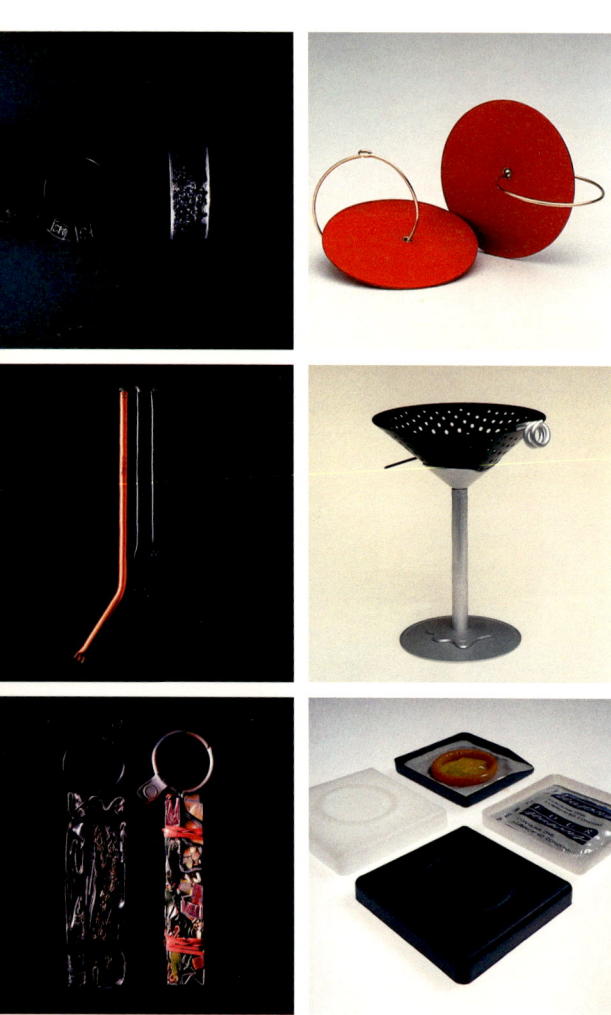

Cohndom doughnut box

tableware

Cohnical phase V   Alessi Cohncave

exhibition 01

...and does it work?

Walkman #1   Microphone   Security pass

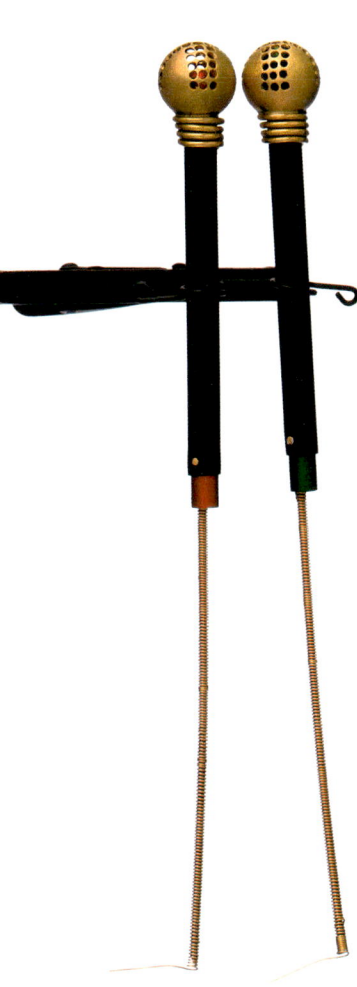

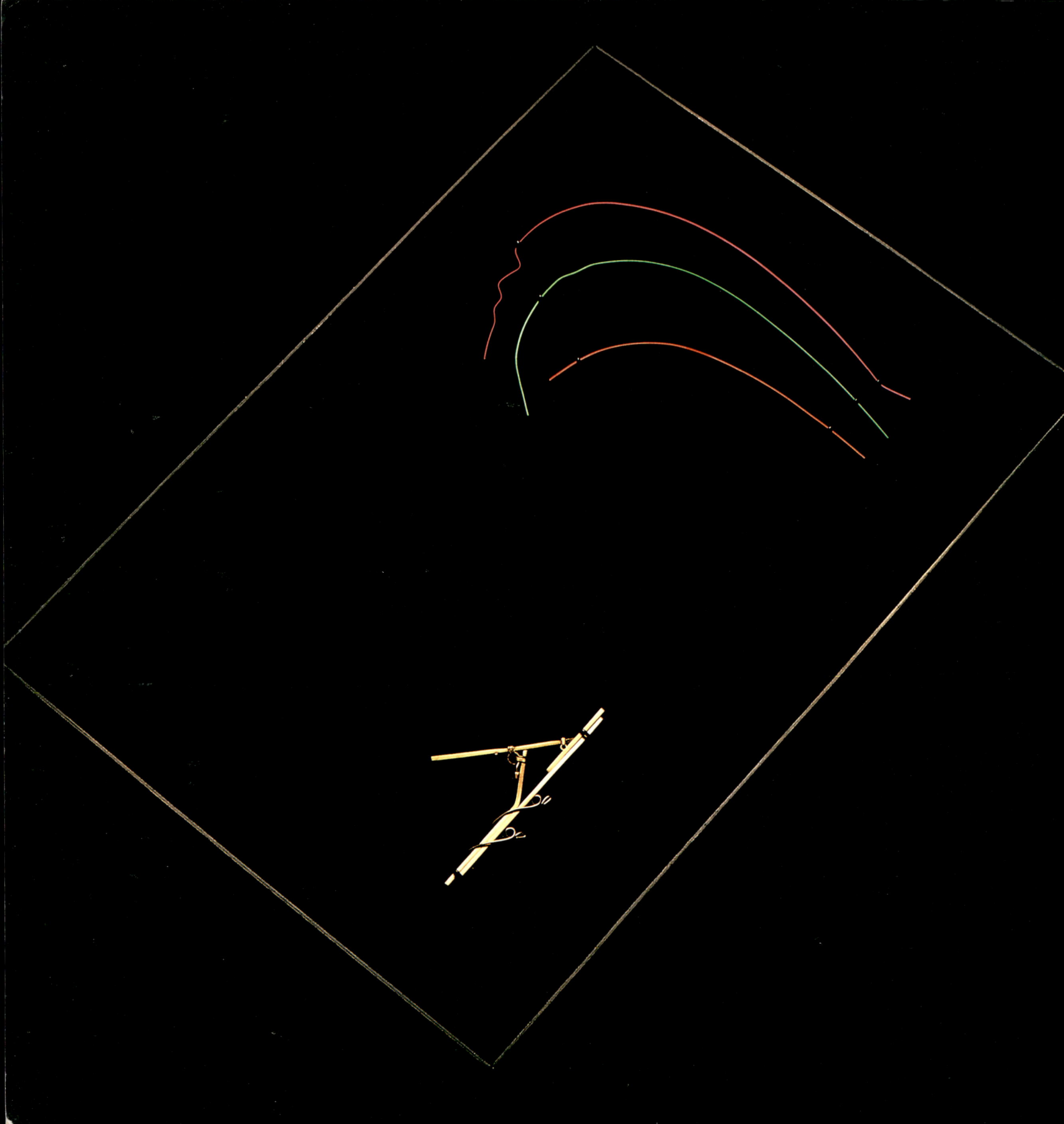

exhibition 02
cosmetic manipulations

Eye piece   Nose piece

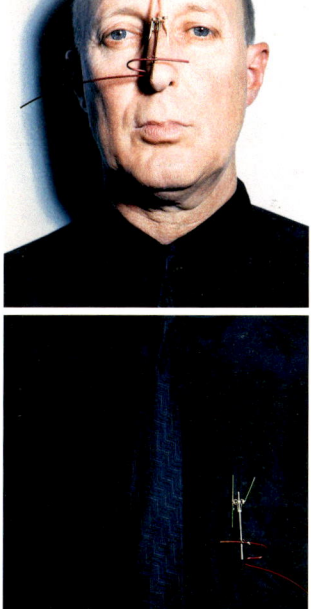

Gibsonia #5   Laliquiana #1

exhibition
05
catch me

exhibition 06
survival habits

Survival kit #2

Susan Cohn

		Born 1952 Australia
	1980 to 2000	Director Workshop 3000 Melbourne
		Represented by Anna Schwartz Gallery (formerly City Gallery)
		185 Flinders Lane Melbourne Victoria Australia Telephone 613 9654 6131 Facsimile 613 9650 5418
Training	1986	Graduate Diploma of Fine Art Gold and Silversmithing (Distinction)
		Royal Melbourne Institute of Technology Victoria
	1980	Diploma of Art, Gold and Silversmithing Royal Melbourne Institute of Technology Victoria
	1971 to 1977	Trained and worked as a graphic designer
Other studies	1998–	Candidate for Doctorate of Fine Art Theory University of New South Wales Sydney
Selected major commissions/awards	1998	Melbourne, Victorian Design Awards, Industrial Design award
	1998	Milan, Centro Studi Alessi *Cohndom* boxes (two versions)
	1990	Milan, Centro Studi Alessi *Cohncave* bowl
	1995	Australia Council Visual Arts/Crafts Board Fellowship grant
	1995	Design Institute of Australia, Hall of Fame
	1988	English Speaking Union, Stuart Devlin National Craft award
Master workshops	1996	20th Anniversary Fellowship, Australian National University Canberra School of Art Glass Workshop
	1995	Alessi Workshop conducted with Dr Alberto Alessi, College of Fine Arts University of NSW Sydney
	1995	Royal College of Art London Gold and Silversmithing
Solo exhibitions	2000	Canberra, National Gallery of Australia *Techno Craft: The Work of Susan Cohn 1980 to 2000*
	1999	Glasgow, Glasgow School of Art *Techno Craft 33.3%*
	1999	Tokyo, Idée Gallery *Cohn*
	1998	Melbourne, Anna Schwartz Gallery *Catch Me*
	1995	Melbourne, Anna Schwartz Gallery *Reflections on A Safe Future*
	1994	Melbourne, Anna Schwartz Gallery *Way Past Real*
	1994	Dunedin New Zealand, FLUXUS *Cosmetic Manipulations*
	1992	Melbourne, City Gallery *Cosmetic Manipulations*
	1989	Melbourne, City Gallery *…and does it work?*
	1989	Tokyo, Shibuya Seibu Loft Styling Gallery
	1988	Sydney, Contemporary Jewellery Gallery
	1987	Melbourne, Christine Abrahams Gallery
	1987	Launceston, The Queen Victoria Museum and Art Gallery
	1984	Melbourne, Devise Gallery
Selected major group exhibitions	1979 to 2000	107 group exhibitions and competitions in Australia, Japan, China, Asia, America and Europe including
	1999	Milan, La Posteria *Make Love with Design*
	1998	Edinburgh, National Museums of Scotland *Jewellery Moves: International Jewellery Exhibition*
		Amsterdam, Galerie Ra *Overseas*
		Singapore, Earl Lu Gallery La Salle-SIA *The Somatic Object*
	1997	Melbourne, National Gallery of Victoria *Cicely and Colin Rigg Craft Award*
		Shanghai China, Shanghai Museum *Contemporary Vessels and Jewels*
		Brisbane, Queensland Art Gallery *Contemporary Vessels and Jewels*
		Munich, Internationalen Handwerksmesse *Schmuck '97*
		Sydney, Ivan Dougherty Gallery *The Somatic Object*
		Taipei Taiwan, National Museum of History *The Somatic Object*
	1996	Amsterdam, Galerie Ra *Jewellery of the Future*
	1995	Melbourne, National Gallery of Victoria *VicHealth National Craft Award*
	1994 to 1995	Craft Victoria, Australian Touring Exhibition *Symmetry Crafts Meet Kindred Trades and Professions*
	1993 to 1994	RMIT and Asialink, Asia Touring Exhibition *Australia Gold*
	1991	Milan, Centro Studi Alessi *Rebus Sic Memory Containers*
		London, Electrum Gallery *20th Anniversary Exhibition*
Selected representation		National Gallery of Australia
		National Gallery of Victoria
		Victoria and Albert Museum, London
		National Museums of Scotland
		Royal College of Art, London
		Alessi Museum, Cruisinallo
		Art Gallery of South Australia
		Powerhouse Museum of Applied Arts and Sciences, Sydney
		Queen Victoria Museum & Art Gallery, Launceston
		Art Gallery of Queensland
		Art Gallery of Western Australia
		Northern Territory Museum of Arts and Sciences
		Jewish Museum of Australia, Melbourne
		Victoria State Collection
		City of Banyule Art Collection
		Private collections

© 1999 National Gallery of Australia
GPO Box 1150, Canberra, ACT 2601
All rights reserved. No part of
this publication may be reproduced,
stored in a retrieval system,
or transmitted in any form or by
any means electronic, mechanical,
photocopying, recording
or otherwise without the prior
permission of the publisher.

Cataloguing-in-publication data.
*Techno Craft: the work
of Susan Cohn 1980 to 2000.*
ISBN 0642 541469
1. Cohn, Susan, 1952– Exhibitions
2. Jewelry – Australia
3. Jewelry making – Australia
I. Cohn, Susan, 1952–
II. National Gallery of Australia
739.270994
Produced by the Publications
Department, National Gallery
of Australia
Designed by Emery Vincent Design
Melbourne
Printed by Toth Bienk & Associates
Melbourne

Susan Cohn
would like to thank
Garry Emery
Jackie Cooper
Bruce James
Kate Gollings
Earl Carter
for their generous
contribution to
this book

Susan Cohn is represented
by Anna Schwartz Gallery

Photography:
Kate Gollings
Earl Carter
John Gollings
Isamu Sawa
Greg Harris
Johannes Kuhnen

Ann Lewis Gold doughnut neckring